A Family in Jamaica

LIBRARY OF CONGRESS CATALOGING IN PUBLICATION DATA

Hubley, John.
   A family in Jamaica.

   Rev. ed. of: Jamaican village. 1982.
   Summary: Describes the life of Dorothy, who lives in
a small village on the north coast of Jamaica.
   1. Jamaica—Social life and customs—Juvenile
literature. 2. Children—Jamaica—Juvenile literature.
[1. Jamaica—Social life and customs] I. Hubley, Penny.
II. Hubley, John. Jamaican village. III. Title.
F1874.H83 1985   972.92   85-6887
ISBN 0-8225-1657-8 (lib. bdg.)

Manufactured in the United States of America

   4   5   6   7   8   9   10   95   94   93   92   91

A Family in Jamaica

John and Penny Hubley

Lerner Publications Company • Minneapolis

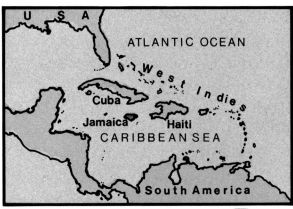

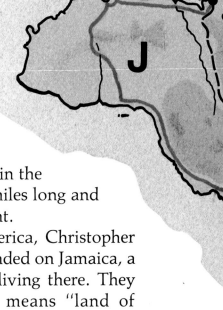

This is Dorothy Samuels. She lives in Cascade, a village near Montego Bay, on the north coast of Jamaica.

Jamaica is one of a group of islands in the Caribbean Sea. Jamaica is almost 150 miles long and is about 50 miles wide at its widest point.

In 1494, on his second trip to America, Christopher Columbus sighted Jamaica. When he landed on Jamaica, a group of people called Arawaks were living there. They called their island Xaymaca, which means "land of wood and water." The name Jamaica comes from this Arawak word.

Columbus, who still thought he had discovered India, called the islands the West Indies and the people Indians.

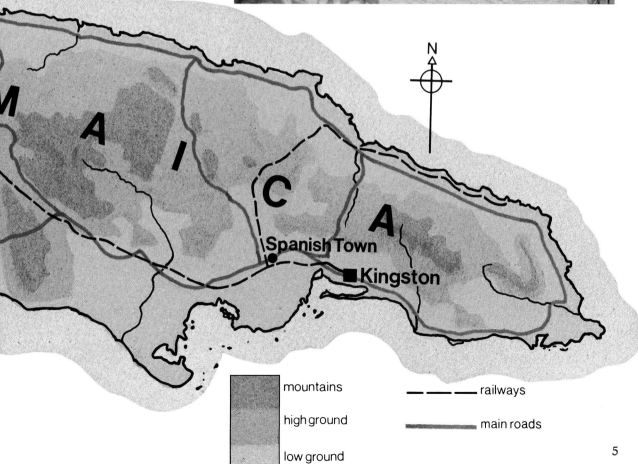

mountains

high ground

low ground

- - - railways

━━━ main roads

Dorothy is ten years old. She lives with her parents, her sister, and her brother. Their house is made of wood and has an iron roof.

The weather is always hot in Jamaica. To catch the breeze, Dorothy's house is built on pillars.

At the front of the house is a big shady porch. Dorothy and her family often sit out there to cool off. From the porch you can see the coconut, orange, and breadfruit trees that grow in the garden. Breadfruit is a large round green fruit that is boiled or baked before eating.

Outside the house is a water faucet. People used to have to collect water from the streams and carry it back home. But now, water is piped to every house in the village.

Dorothy's sister is a college student in Kingston, the capital of Jamaica. She is home on vacation for a month but must still study. She studies in the living room, which is decorated with pictures and cards. Some of the cards come from relatives who live in the United States or in England.

When she is home, Dorothy's sister makes lunch. The family has a gas stove. They buy the gas in large metal containers. Some Jamaican families cook on a kerosene stove or over a wood fire.

Cascade is a small village of about two thousand people. It was once larger, and a big market was held there every week. Now more people work in the towns, and Cascade is not as busy as it once was.

The five grocery stores in the village sell such items as canned food, cookies, soft drinks, and soap. Sometimes the villagers bring vegetables and fruit from their gardens for the shopkeeper to sell.

The small village library is open every afternoon. Children often stop in after school to read or check out books.

Next to the library is a health clinic where mothers bring their children to be examined by the nurse. There is also a bank and a post office in the village.

Each Sunday, Dorothy's family goes to church. Dorothy goes to Sunday school. Before the service starts, the adults like to listen to the children sing.

Dorothy goes to the village school. The school is in a modern building, and children from all the nearby villages go to school there.

Dorothy started school when she was five years old. Next year, when she is eleven, she will take an important test. If she passes it, she will be able to go to the high school in Montego Bay.

Dorothy likes school. She wants to go to college when she is older, like her sister does.

School children in Jamaica wear uniforms. Dorothy's uniform is blue, but each school has a different uniform.

Some of the girls in Dorothy's school have their hair braided in fancy styles. This keeps them cool. The girls get their mothers or their friends to braid their hair. Some of the hairstyles can take hours to do.

Dorothy's older brother, Martin, also goes to the village school. After school, he earns extra money by running errands for people in the village. He has made a wooden cart and uses it to carry goods. The cart has a steering wheel and lights and bumpers, just like a truck.

11

Like most of the people in Cascade, the Samuels are farmers. They have their own farm, which Dorothy's grandfather runs.

One of their crops is the yam plant, which grows as a vine propped up by a stick. The yams grow under the ground, like potatoes.

To plant yams, the farmers dig up the soil and make mounds of earth. Then they place one yam into each mound.

Farming is hard work, and everyone is glad to take an hour's break at noon. Each worker is given a cooked meal as part of his pay.

Each day, Dorothy's grandfather checks the vines to make sure that they are healthy. When the yams are ready to be harvested, the vines die. Then the yams are dug up from the earth.

Most of the farms in Cascade are small, less than ten acres. But in that space, the farmers grow many different crops.

In addition to growing yams, the Samuels family grows coconuts, bananas, cocoa, potatoes, oranges, avocados, and other kinds of fruits and vegetables.

Dorothy's family eats some of the food grown on the farm. They store most of the yams and potatoes to eat in the months after the harvest. The rest of the fruit and vegetables are sold to people in the village or at the market in Montego Bay.

Dorothy's mother makes cocoa from her own cocoa beans. When the cocoa pods are ripe, they are cut down. Then the beans are taken out of the pods and dried in the sun. Most of the beans are sold to a factory that makes cocoa powder and chocolate.

The Samuels have cows, but they have to keep them tied up so they don't eat the crops. When a cow has a calf, the family keeps it for about a year and then sells the calf to a local butcher.

The Samuels drink the milk from their cows. They are lucky, since there is very little fresh milk in Jamaica. Most people use powdered milk or canned milk.

Dorothy's uncle, who lives on a nearby farm, keeps goats for their milk and pigs and chickens for meat. People from the surrounding villages often come to his farm to buy from him. He weighs the animals to decide the price he will charge. He also keeps bees and sells the honey they make.

Sometimes Dorothy's family has lunch at her uncle's farm. Dorothy's favorite Jamaican dish is jerk pork. The pork is spiced and cooked slowly on a fire of green wood. The smoky fire gives the meat its special taste.

Jerk pork was first cooked over two hundred years ago. At that time, the sailors who came to Jamaica had spent many weeks at sea eating ship's rations. They wanted fresh food, so they caught wild pigs to eat. Because there was no dry firewood, the sailors had to cut down trees and cook the pork on green wood.

Jamaica is famous for its sugar. Three-fourths of the sugar made in Jamaica is sent to other countries. At the same time, Jamaica must import many other kinds of food, because the country cannot grow as much food as the people need.

The tall sugar canes look very different from the sugar bought in a store. At harvest time, the canes are cut down with a cutlass. This tool has a sharp blade and is used for pruning and digging as well as harvesting.

Before the cane is harvested, it is burned to remove the dry leaves. This makes it easier to cut. Cutting cane is still very hard work, and the workers get covered with black ash.

When the cane has been cut, a grabbing machine picks it up and loads it onto a wagon. The cut cane is taken to the sugar factory. At the factory, the cane is crushed to release the juice inside. This cane juice is put through several more steps to turn it into raw sugar, which is a light brown color. Some of the raw sugar is made into rum, a liquor, and some is refined to become white sugar.

The sugar cane is harvested from January through August. During the rest of the year, the workers plant more sugar and clean and repair the machines in the factory.

Every Saturday there is a big market in Montego Bay. Dorothy's mother and grandmother go to the market very early in the morning. They sell fruit and vegetables grown on the family farm.

The weekly market is colorful and busy. Dorothy's mother and grandmother put out their fruit and vegetables in the same place every week. They know all the other traders and chat with them as they work. Sometimes Dorothy comes too.

The traders at the market are all women. Jamaicans have a special name for women traders. They call them *higglers*.

People from Montego Bay and the nearby villages come to the market every week. They meet their friends and buy their fruit and vegetables.

Ackee is one of the most popular kinds of fruit at the market. It is the national fruit of Jamaica. Ackee grows on trees and is poisonous until it splits open. Then the yellow part inside can be eaten, but the black seeds cannot. Ackee tastes like a mixture of chestnuts and scrambled eggs. With saltfish, it is the Jamaican national dish.

1 Green bananas	6 Spinach	11 Cabbage
2 Yams	7 Limes	12 Avocado
3 Sweet potatoes	8 Coconut	13 Tomatoes
4 Plantain	9 Turnips	14 Papayas
5 Sugar cane	10 Squash	15 Carrots

Montego Bay is a busy town. In addition to the weekly market, it has lots of stores, movie theaters, banks, restaurants, and offices. People from Cascade often go into Montego Bay. They usually ride the bus, which drives along the twisting road through the hills. Some people make the trip every day to go to work or to school.

The stores in Cascade are small and don't have much variety, so the villagers also shop in Montego Bay. They buy such items as clothes, shoes, furniture, and books there. The supermarkets in Montego Bay also sell many kinds of foods that aren't available in Cascade.

Dorothy enjoys going on trips to Montego Bay. When her mother has finished work at the market, they look around in the big stores. As a special treat, Dorothy sometimes has ice cream or a sky juice. Sky juice is made of sweet fruit juice and ice. It comes in a plastic bag or cup.

Cascade has no doctor. The health clinic sends people who are sick to the hospital in Montego Bay, which is large and fairly new.

Many people from other countries come to Jamaica
on vacation. They like the sunshine, the beautiful beaches,
and the mountains. Most tourists stay in the big hotels
near the Caribbean Sea.

Many Jamaicans work in the offices, kitchens, and restaurants of these hotels. Some of the people from Dorothy's village work as waiters and cooks.

Hardly any tourists go to Cascade. But in Montego Bay, Dorothy often sees the tourists looking for presents to take home. They buy straw hats, baskets, T-shirts, and wooden carvings. The visitors can even watch while some of the souvenirs are being made.

When Columbus discovered Jamaica, he claimed it for Spain. The Spanish people who came to Jamaica made slaves out of the Arawak people who had been living there and also brought slaves from Africa to Jamaica. Almost all of the Arawak died from disease and from being worked so hard.

The British invaded Jamaica about 200 years later. The British who settled in Jamaica were farmers and grew sugar to send to Great Britain. These farmers needed workers for their sugar plantations, so they continued to bring slaves from Africa to work on the farms.

Some of the sugar farmers became very wealthy and built grand stone houses. These houses are now tourist attractions.

The slaves wanted to be free. Some of them ran into the mountains or tried to fight for their freedom. They were named Maroons, from the Spanish word *cimarron*, which means "untamed."

Some Europeans felt that the slaves should be free, but others wanted to keep them enslaved. In 1834, the British Parliament passed a law that freed the slaves. This happened 25 years before Abraham Lincoln signed the Emancipation Proclamation, which freed the slaves in the United States.

Jamaica was a British colony until 1962, when it became an independent nation. The capital of this new country is Kingston, a city with modern stores, offices, factories, and streets full of traffic.

The Influence of Africa

Ninety percent of the people who live in Jamaica have ancestors who came from Africa. The blacks were brought to Jamaica mainly from the west coast of Africa and represent many different tribes and cultures. It is not surprising that both Jamaica's language and music show an African influence.

Although the official language of Jamaica is English, many people who live in Jamaica also speak what they call "Jamaica talk." Jamaica talk is a mixture of English and African words. Here are some Jamaica talk words and their meanings:

nyam: eat
boonoonoonoos: happiness and delight
talawah: strong and courageous
duppy: ghost

Jamaican music combines African rhythms with European, mostly British, kinds of melodies. A variety of instruments, including several kinds of drums, can be heard in Jamaican music. Reggae, a style of music now popular all over the world, originated in Jamaica.

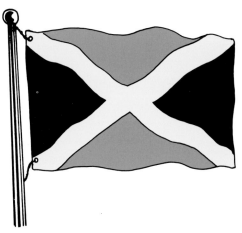

Facts about Jamaica

Capital: Kingston

Official Language: English

Form of Money: the Jamaican dollar

Area: 4,411 square miles
(10,991 square kilometers)
   Jamaica is slightly smaller than the state of
   Connecticut.

Population: about 2.5 million people

NORTH
AMERICA

Jamaica

SOUTH
AMERICA

EUROPE

A S I A

AFRICA

AUSTRALIA

Families the World Over

Some children in foreign countries live like you do. Others live very differently. In these books, you can meet children from all over the world. You'll learn about their games and schools, their families and friends, and what it's like to grow up in a faraway land.

An Aboriginal Family	A Family in Hong Kong	A Family in Nigeria
An Arab Family	A Family in Hungary	A Family in Norway
A Family in Australia	A Family in India	A Family in Pakistan
A Family in Bolivia	A Family in Ireland	A Family in Peru
A Family in Brazil	A Kibbutz in Israel	A Family in Singapore
A Family in Chile	A Family in Italy	A Family in South Korea
A Family in China	A Family in Jamaica	A Family in Sri Lanka
A Family in Egypt	A Family in Japan	A Family in Sudan
A Family in England	A Family in Kenya	A Family in Taiwan
An Eskimo Family	A Family in Liberia	A Family in Thailand
A Family in France	A Family in Mexico	A Family in West Germany
	A Family in Morocco	A Zulu Family

Lerner Publications Company, 241 First Avenue North, Minneapolis, Minnesota 55401